ARMSTRONG
ROAD

Kirk McKenna

WESTBOW
P R E S S®
A DIVISION OF THOMAS NELSON
& ZONDERVAN

WestBow Press books may be ordered through booksellers or by contacting:

WestBow Press
A Division of Thomas Nelson & Zondervan
1663 Liberty Drive
Bloomington, IN 47403
www.westbowpress.com
844-714-3454

Scripture taken from the King James Version of the Bible.

ISBN: 978-1-6642-4846-5 (sc)
ISBN: 978-1-6642-4847-2 (e)

Print information available on the last page.

WestBow Press rev. date: 11/10/2021

The steps of a good man are ordered by the Lord: and he delighteth in his way. Though he fall, he shall not be utterly cast down: for the Lord upholdeth him with his hand. I have been young and now I am old: yet have I not seen the righteous forsaken, nor his seed begging bread.

—Psalm 37:23-25 (KJV)

CONTENTS

INTRODUCTION

THE FOLLOWING IS AN ACCOUNT OF SOME REAL-LIFE EVENTS that took place in my life when I felt that almighty God was with me in some unique and powerful ways. I was not able to share everything or every incident, but I touch on memorable ones in hopes that they may help or encourage readers.

FOREWORD

J UST OFF THE RIVER ROAD IN GLOUCESTER WAS A DIRT SIDE ROAD surrounded by forests and fields.

Mike Powell and Gary Wand took us residents for walks to Armstrong Road to get some exercise and fresh air. We would sing while we were walking or sometimes just chat among ourselves.

After a few months, I would wake up in the late hours while everyone was asleep and go outside unnoticed by the night security watch and walk by myself down River Road toward Manotick and on Armstrong Road. There was no lights; it was complete darkness except for the stars or moon on clear nights. It was my go-to place to be alone. I liked the quietness and tranquility of it. At times, all I heard were crickets and frogs, and all I saw were fireflies. It was much like when I lived in the country for many years. I enjoyed walking after dark and even in the rain. There was just something peaceful about it.

CHAPTER 1

1989

BEING YOUNG IS EVERYTHING—BEING CAREFREE, HAVING A free spirit, and so on. Never thinking about yesterday or worrying about tomorrow; all that matters is the moment. The overwhelming excitement of energy and peace and free spirit is on you and in you and around you.

It is yours alone.

Embrace it and hang onto it as long as you can; it is a pinnacle like no other.

Keep your heart open and your spirit free.

Because the darkness comes in like a giant wave.

Keep your faith and your mind and your spirit free.

Be strong and rise above it all.
Forever keep your spirit free.

I was young—nineteen—and I was enjoying life. I had a small but close circle of guy friends. They were my buddies—comrades I might say. We lived every day as if it were our last. We had a lot of fun; we were adventurous and loved excitement. We did not always make wise decisions, but who does at that age?

We were good kids. The 1980s were good years. We were just enjoying every moment, and we loved to laugh. Sometimes, we would go fishing or camp out for the night by a lake or river. Or we would go to the theater and see a good movie, but we'd goof around in there and sometimes almost get kicked out because of the noise, laughter, and craziness.

Sometimes, we would go the roller-skating arena, where there was a big MuchMusic or MTV video screen playing videos and loud music of the time. It was a blast. Other times, we would have small house parties, go to the bars and clubs and drink into the late hours of the night, take taxis all over the place, and shoot off fireworks. We loved pulling pranks on each other, and we all got turns at that. We laughed all the time. Even if we were all broke, that did not stop us; we were young and enjoying our youth. Those were the best times in my life.

It was August 1989 when everything started to fall apart for me. I was at a house party where the host decided she wanted to have a seance. I was not quite comfortable with it, but I was there making jokes and almost mocking it. It might have been that encounter, or my heavy drinking at the time, or sleepless nightlife fun, but whatever it was, things abruptly came to a halt for me. I was quickly removed from the equation and from my friends and the life I was enjoying.

I was overtaken suddenly with acute anxiety, fear, and a sense of impending doom. It gripped me hard and shook me to my core. I was a bundle of nerves, and I developed agoraphobia. I was shaken and overcome, and I did not know what was wrong or was going on with me. I wanted it to stop, though, and I wanted my life back. I was desperate to be free.

I even ran into a church one evening during the service screaming for help. The pastor and elders laid hands on me and prayed for me. My stepdad and mom and many people were present, perhaps much to their embarrassment. I also had a visit from the pastor and his wife, and she made tea to calm me and prayed for me.

We took a trip to Brampton, Ontario, to the teen challenge center. The pastor had recommended that my stepdad take me there because they did not know what else to do with me, and my condition was difficult to watch and cope with. I did not stay at the teen challenge facility because I was full of anxiety and could not relax. I stayed with a brother of mine and his family for a short time, and then I ended up staying with a retired couple in town. They were good Christian people and read the Bible and prayed together every day. The wife cooked breakfast every morning; it was so good. Her husband played the guitar and sang sometimes. A few times, a pastor friend of theirs came by, and he sat and talked with me and prayed for me. During the few months I was there, the older gentlemen ministered to me and passed on some wise knowledge and things to me.

I had an aunt who resided in the city of Ottawa, and her next-door neighbor was on the board of directors of a men's rehabilitation or recovery home called Harvest House Ministries. My mom and my aunt were talking, and this is how it all came about. After some paperwork, I ended up going there on October 26, 1989. Some people were opposed to it, but I knew that things could not go on as they were and that I needed to go somewhere.

My mom drove me there. I met Jack, who was the head chef in the home's kitchen. I also met with Larry Seelye, who was to be my counselor. I was scared, but my life was already upside down and uncertain, and I thought, *How much worse could it get at this point?* I was a burden on my parents and some of my siblings. The older couple couldn't take care of me anymore (though I will be forever grateful to them). My friends at the time did not understand me at all and just carried on without me, and things were never the same with them. I sure missed them, but I wanted my life to get back to normal or at least what I'd thought was normal.

Harvest House was a Christ-centered alcohol and drug and dependency recovery and treatment program for men. The program was one year in length. This was to be my new home for a while. It was in an old school building along River Road; it had a farmhouse and a chalet as well for residents. River Road connected Ottawa to the town of Manotick.

I was assigned a room in the main building. There were bunk beds in each room. We ate in the cafeteria, and we attended PD (personal development) meetings in a big room. We'd sit in a circle and sometimes prayed. Other times, confrontations took place between residents or between staff and residents, or we'd have discussions about the program. We'd talk about likes or dislikes or maybe the food there. It was place where we could rant, vent, and share about our lives or anything else, or we could just be quiet, relax, and listen. There was a room at the far end specifically for morning prayer meetings.

CHAPTER 4

Guarded

I
T WAS NICE TO BE BACK HOME. IT WAS A FRESH FEELING. SOME people asked me where I had been; they hadn't seen me in a long time. I told them about some of my experiences and how I had recovered from anxiety and a alcohol addiction. I spoke at one school to teens about the dangers of alcohol and drugs and the importance of a relationship with Christ.

It was nice to see my old friends again though it was different. Life just carried on. I felt good, and I knew God was with me because I had been through a lot and had endured a lot. I had graduated from a one-year program and stayed an additional four months as a junior staff counselor and night security. I felt I had paid my dues, and I was at peace. I was guarded by a higher power.

I have been passing on what I had learned during that time.

- Start your day morning or night whatever your situation by confessing any sins to God and ask his forgiveness.
- Thank God for your blessings and praise him.
- Pray for family and friends.
- Pray for any enemies you might have.
- Pray for any needs you have.
- Talk to God frequently.
- Plead the blood of Jesus over yourself and your home.
- Recite Revelation 12:11 and personalize it.
- Put on the armor of God as in Ephesians 6:10–18 and read it out loud.
- Put on the cloak of zeal (Isaiah 59:17)
- Put on the ornament of a meek, quiet, and teachable spirit (1 Peter 3:5–6).
- Take the glory of the Lord as your rearguard (Isaiah 58:8).
- Recite Psalm 91, and then personalize it and the whole chapter.
- Keep in mind that you are guarded by God's armor and his grace and his angels.
- Make time for God, and protect yourself so you will be equipped to be guarded against our adversary and spiritual attacks.

- Do not worry; even if you do not feel it, God is standing with you and helping you. We all have days when we feel alone and misunderstood.
- We are not alone.
- We are guarded.

CHAPTER 5

Mariners Inn Incident

I n October 1992, I was residing on Market Street in the old post office that had been converted into apartments. It was a stone building and was at least a hundred years old.

Jack Gleeson, an older man who lived down the hall, was my neighbor (and later my good friend). His father and some of his uncles, who had come to Canada in 1912, were supposed to be aboard the *Titanic* but had missed it because one of the brothers became sick; they cancelled that trip and came over later that year from Ireland. What a twist of fate.

They told me many stories including about eighteen-year-old Eric Hutcheson waving to them when they were kids and going off to war. They named a school and a road after him back in Smiths Falls.

One day, I read an ad about a church seminar concerning end-time events, and it made me curious. It was to be held in a conference room at the Mariners Inn Hotel down by the Rideau River in town.

I showed up there and listened to some soft Christian songs that were playing. A speaker started talking about the four horsemen in Revelation 6 and what they symbolized. He ended the meeting by asking if anybody wanted to become saved and if so to bow his or her head and pray. I sat there for few minutes. I heard a woman telling her daughter that this was some kind of a cult. I was not sure what to think of it all.

I attended the next meeting. I walked into the conference room and saw people seated and facing the front where the screen was. Nobody was moving; it was as if they were in a trance. On the screen up front, I saw the words *birth pains* and a passage from Matthew or Luke flashing continuously. A man was walking around and placing sheets of paper face-down on the chairs next to everybody. I felt a small breeze behind me, and the paper beside me blew off and onto the floor behind me. I looked around; nobody else's paper had blown off the chairs beside them.

A minute later, the large ceiling light and glass shade directly over me came crashing down and shattered on the floor right beside me with a loud bang and crash. Strangely, it was as if nobody sitting near me even noticed that or looked my way.

A man came along with a broom and dustpan and quietly and quickly swept up the debris and was gone. It was so bizarre.

Despite what had just happened, I sat through the seminar until the end. They had their prayer and afterward had some books and literature for sale and some refreshments and food. I did not have any money to purchase any of the books or literature about their religion of the four horsemen and the Sabbath Day and other topics. I asked the woman at the desk selling the books what religion was this, and she replied the Seventh Day Adventists. I said, "I've never heard of it."

I left shortly after that. I was beginning to think that maybe this was some kind of a cult or something; it was just not sitting right in my gut, and of course the incident of the paper and ceiling light and shade … I was thinking it was God or an angel telling me to get out of there.

I was at a grocery store a few days later and saw the pastor of the Seventh Day Adventist church, who saw me. I tried to avoid him, but he came up to me and started to speak to me in a friendly way. He asked me why I hadn't come back to the seminars or the church. For some reason, I saw something evil in his eyes as if he was angry at me, and that scared me a bit. I told him straight out but nicely that I would not be returning and wanted nothing to do with it. I left.

My heart was pounding. I was shaken by that encounter. The man had spooked me. Somehow, the pastor and the evangelist found out where I lived, and a few days later, they came to my place. I invited them in, and we spoke for a few minutes. I had a plaque on my wall of the serenity prayer and praying hands; the evangelist stared at it briefly and nervously for some reason. He looked at me and said, "God is going to use you, son." They shook my hand and left. I never saw them again.

Months later, I was up late one night and turning TV channels and came across the evangelist who had given the seminar and who had come to my home. He was preaching the gospel. I was surprised and of course I tuned in and watched and listened to him.

A few years later, I heard that he had passed away.

Whatever his religion was—I didn't understand it as I had been taught the Bible and Christianity's foundational beliefs in a different way—we did have one thing in common; we both believed that Jesus Christ was the Son of God and that He rose from the dead and was the only way to God. I did respect him; I have to believe I will see this man again in the next life.

It was encounter that I will not ever forget.

CHAPTER 6

The Immortal Jesus Christ

A LMOST 2,000 YEARS HAVE PASSED, BUT THE NAME OF JESUS Christ is still mentioned today. Many people have come and gone through the centuries; the great and small have done significant things to change history, but no other name has lived to stand the test of time. It is heard every day in churches, religious programs on TV, at weddings and funerals, and when some people swear.

History accounts for Jesus's birth; everything is either BC (before Christ) or AD (*anno domini*, Latin for "in the year of the Lord"). This still-popular person made such an impact on the world. Christmas, Good Friday, and Easter mark his birth, death, and resurrection.

Of all the gods or goddesses, religious figures and religions of the past and present both mythical or real such as Zeus, Hercules, the Titans, Baal, Diana, Buddha, Muhammed, Karma, Hare Krishnas, Jesuits, and popes, none have outlived or outdone Jesus's magnitude and charisma. Many historians, archaeologists, evolutionists, and even some theologians say that in the Old Testament, from Genesis to Malachi, there was a stretch of about 4,000 years at the end of which was a 400-year period known as the silent years though they were not that silent. The Persians ruled, and Alexander the Great had his reign and then was defeated by the Roman Empire, which brings us to about the time Christ was born.

During those years, it was the custom of the Jews and other God-fearing people to sacrifice lambs to cover their sins. It was the way to get off the hook and start clean again. A lamb was chosen because it was innocent and frail and it was white, signifying purity. The Ten Commandments were the laws passed from God to Moses, but after Christ came, he broke the curse of the law by laying down his life so people would not have to continue this ritual. He became the ultimate sacrifice, and that is why he bears one of the many names so often heard—the Lamb of God. He was the last resource to bridge the gap between God and humankind.

The Father, the Son, and the Holy Ghost are one; though they are separate living persons or spirits, they are one together in perfect unison.

Many people have different names or nicknames, but does anybody have as many as Jesus Christ does? Not in any specific order, here they are.

Jesus Christ

Lamb of God

Alpha and Omega

Beginning and End

First and Last

I AM

Lord

Savior

Redeemer

Good Shepherd

Son of God

Holy One

Lion of the Tribe of Judah

Mediator

Son of man

Son of David

Author and Finisher of our faith

Bright and Morning Star

Lily of the Valley

Living One

All-Powerful One

Kings of Kings

Lord of Lords

Is

Was

Rock

Word of God

God

Advocate

Capstone

Master

Light of the World

Only begotten Son

True Light

Almighty

Selah

Bread of Life

Resurrection and the Life

King of Israel

King of the Jews

Man of sorrows

Everlasting King

True God (44)

Lord of Sabaoth

Lord of Sabbath

Rabbi

Judge of all

The Way

The Truth

The Life

Mighty One of Israel

Bridegroom

Head of the Church

Teacher

Horn of Salvation

Revealer of Mysteries

Gods of Gods

Faithful and True

Consuming Fire

Nazarene

Messiah

Emmanuel

True Vine

Spirit of Truth

Root of David

He that Liveth

First-begotten of the Dead

Faithful

Faithful Witness

Prince of the Kings and Earth

The Beginning of the Creation of God

Holy and True

The Lord of Hosts

God almighty

El Shaddai

Jehovah

Jehovah-Jireh

Jehovah-Rapha

Jehovah-Nissi

Jehovah-shalom

Jehovah-Tsur (82)

Jehovah-Roi

Jehovah-Mekaddeskum

Jehovah-Tsidkenu

Jehovah-Elyon

Jehovah-Joshua

Jehovah-Elohim

Jehovah-Shammah

God of Abraham, Isaac, and Jacob

God of Shadrach, Meshach, and Abednego

Man from Galilee

There are probably many more names he is recognized by. He accomplished much during his short life on earth. He began his ministry when he was thirty and was crucified at age thirty-three. He helped out so many people who were having problems. He healed people of their illnesses and performed all kinds of miracles so that people would believe he was for real. He tried to teach people the right way to live. He spoke to people in parables (riddles) about the secrets to life and his kingdom (where he came from) and how they could get there by following certain and simple guidelines.

Jesus had another side to him where he would withdraw himself from people and talk or pray to his Father sometimes for a few hours or sometimes all night. One time, he did it for forty days and forty nights. He prayed for himself, his disciples, and even for future generations.

He cared for the Jewish community and the Gentiles alike. He wanted everyone to hear his message and come to the knowledge of who he was.

Some of the Jewish leaders of that day including Sadducees, scribes, and Pharisees considered him a threat to their laws and views on religion and would try to trick him in their line of questioning, but they never could; he would turn the story around and bewilder them, and they would get angry. They even tried to kill him a few times.

He felt everything that everyday people felt—happiness, sadness, loneliness, hurt, pain, and even death. He was loved by many and hated by many, a lot like today.

Though he had done nothing wrong, his own people, the Jews, had him put to death by orders of the Roman governor, Pontius Pilate, who had a thief released in his place a lot like today when a friend is sold out or stabbed in the back for no reason. Of course we know the rest of the story; he came back to life three days later and appeared to his disciples a few times in a spirit form and then ascended to his home above. He cared enough for humanity to do all that. His message was simple—Believe in me and you shall have life eternal. His promise was that he would always be with his true believers and come back for them at the end of the world.

Even today, people all over the map are hungry and not just for food; they are looking for something and are never satisfied with what they have. A lot like in times when Christ was on earth, people still look to leaders such as politicians, doctors, musicians, lawyers, and religious figures for the answers or the cure. A lot of people also look for it in alcohol, drugs, money, sex, cults, physics, relationships, and even dead icons.

People want to be happy, and they want fulfillment to fill the void they feel inside. Jesus Christ has been gone from this earth for 2,000 years now, and the majority of people you ask will tell you he is dead. He is not dead; he rose from the dead. He is immortal. He is alive just as he ever was back in biblical times. He is the answer for the all the world's problems; he is the only answer. He was, he is, and he is to come.

CHAPTER 7

My Quest

MY QUEST IN THIS LIFE NOW BESIDES THE OBVIOUS THINGS
Is to search out my inner soul
To seek diligently my real role
I know without a doubt
That a higher power plays a big part
Trying to connect with the supreme being
Can be difficult but very smart
Forces of evil and good
Are endless of nature's cause
To separate the sheep from the goats
For that I can pause

I know only one thing for certain
When I die and leave this space
Jesus Christ, the son of God
I will meet Him
Face to face

CONCLUSION

I HOPE THIS MANUSCRIPT HAS BEEN INTERESTING AND HAS inspired or given you a spark of hope and encouragement no matter who you are or your background or beliefs.

No matter what our situations look like or how impossible or hopeless they seem, nothing is impossible with God. He can turn the tide on any situation and have favor on us because he loves us.

ACKNOWLEDGMENTS

Reverend Hilts

Joe Henderson

Pastor Paul and Shirley Henderson

George Morrison

Tony Hendrix

David Wilkerson

Don and Theresa Ferguson

Adele Morrison (my mom, to whom I am forever grateful and love so much)

Betty Haines (Jerry and Stephen and Suzan)

Dave Joynt

John Mayville

Cory Mayville

Bill and Catherine Main

Andrew Main

Janice Frasor

Mike Powell

Gary Wand

Larry Seelye

Bob Ware

Jeff Clifford

Mario

Bill Krakana

Mel Goddard

Charlie Keeping

Mike Mckegney

Rene (a comrade who taught me how to play a Cat Stevens song)

Gabe from Wawa, Ontario

Dallas Holm (whom I saw live in concert and prayed for me after ward)

Peter McKenna (my brother)

The music of Keith Green and Amy Grant

Steve Russo

Chris Viau

Kevin Doucette

Craig and Sarah Code

All the band members of Siloam

Danny Wise

Danny Roy

Darren Coffin

Brian Gortler

Danny Nurse

Brad Giftkins

Hugh McComb

Andy Westwater

Reverend Henry Fyerhand

Pastor Steven and Janet Ching

Pastor Clay Hilton

Bob Thiebodeau

Martin (my Irish friend)

Barry Jodin

Earl McNulty

To all who have helped me along the way and with my walk with Christ, I thank you sincerely.

Printed in the United States
by Baker & Taylor Publisher Services